THE AGE OF STEEL

Rudi Matić

PASCAL EDITION

THE AGE OF STEEL

A Pascal Editions Book / May 2018
Copyright @ 2018 by Rudi Matić

First Edition Published by
Pascal Editions
Rochester New York

Layout and Cover Design by Pascal Editions

This is a book of poetry. Names, characters, places and incidents are either the products of the author's imagination or are used fictitiously or metaphorically. Any resemblance to actual persons, living or dead, events or locales is entirely coincidental.

All Rights Reserved. Except for use in review, the reproduction or utilization of this work in whole or in part in any form by any electronic, mechanical or other means now known or hereafter invented, is prohibited without the written permission of the author or publisher.

Za
Tomo Matić
i
Natasha Fyodorovna Ptahina Matić

Dragi moj otac i majka

CONTENTS

Bloch	1
Deluge	2
The Racquetball Players	3
Exilic	4
My Centuries	5
Dresden	6
Ascending Stairs	8
Valkyrie	9
I Am A Bat	10
Trinity	12
Collage of Beautiful	13
Figure	14
Susan Sontag	15
Countenance	16
Cold Bounty	17
Unaussprechlingen	18
Twelve Lines	20
Bridal	21
A Few Moments To Breathe	22
'Lucifer, Abrupt'	24
Catastrophe	25
The Exterminator	26
There	27
The Abstracted Man	28
Ashen Day	29
Kek Joking	30
Dare	32
Extinguished	33
Gossamer Redcurrant	34
Consummation	36
Far From Me	37
Downfall	38
Metropoli	39
An Arc Of Time	40
Ophelia's Scissors	41
Genug	42

Material For Your Art	*43*
Shadowfall	*44*
Reki	*45*
Serpents Of History	*46*
Red Cities	*47*
Les Enfants Du Paradis	*48*
Archaic Sonnet	*58*
Crude Spade Face	*59*
Rainy Day	*60*
Autumnal	*62*
Victoriana Autumn	*63*
Trawling The Absolute	*64*
A Whiteness	*65*
What We Did	*66*
The Coming Storm	*67*
In The Albers Room	*68*
Displacements	*69*
Ravens Flock	*70*
The Stars For A While Stopped Shining	*71*
Hands of Heaven	*72*
Slapstick Nothingness	*73*
How This Sadness Came To Be Persistent	*74*
Imperium	*75*
Figures Atop The Reichstag	*76*
No Exit	*77*
Stare	*78*
The Inner Life	*79*
The Long Migration	*80*
The Pantomime Erodes	*81*
Collected Silences	*82*
War In The Age Of Intelligent Machines	*83*
My Human Form	*84*
Zero Point	*85*
One Day	*86*
Ostsektor	*87*
Timelike Curves	*114*

BLOCH

The presence of radiance you could not see
Still ravages aesthetics. Twisting wings,
Like startled kanji scrawled on scrolls of snow
As cold and colder than your Leipzig streets,
Lunge into evening as though joyous tors;
Though all you did, all you could do, was stare.

The gesture of your writing neared such peaks.
Ascending the cool rainfall of ancillae,
You fell, pale, upwards toward that terrible rebus;
But the post box, the silver age, were closed,
And could hear nothing, the abandoned casements
Had no recall, and time did what it wanted.

Some mistake such termini for shores.
But waking from waking you could still remember
Birds circling above the ice-strewn seas;
Solace from dread; that darkness will be healed.

DELUGE

Enter the new economy of the drowned:
Hammering at the finite, relentless in transformation,
Chasm of *vita brevis*, opiates;
Nothing above, below, before, within;
Perpetuum mobile whirling to the end.
"Hold fast: *après nous le déluge!*" And after the deluge?
Ordure of reckoning. Those who have sensed
The Athenian, the Stoic, aftertastes
Of order and elevation, felt
The graze of Apollo, may hallucinate
Pity displacing history; but wake
Among the harnessed.
The terminable feral. Turn your back.
The battles are over. Only the pillage remains.

THE RACQUETBALL PLAYERS

We act the sleek hawk world in flight. The kill.
Trajectory. Concentration. Stalk and grip.
We are aware we are the strike we will,
The microsecond where no pause erodes;
Else pirouettes shattered at a wall's rank slap.
Sometimes a tendon or a wrist explodes:
Unanswerable backhands, curt Z-shots,
Indulge no qualm, no hesitance. Here ease rots.
Bullet slants burst, zigzag, tilt, wheel and hook.
We prey and twist within our blank cube. There,
Performance effects, transcends, outcome. For if
Acts have no meaning save what one confers,
One must confer them. Seize them. Strive. Provoke.

EXILIC

Such days! The wind waltzes, the rain drums;
Stars sparkle in the same old way; time yawns.
Era of slaughterhouses, where've you fled,
Stranding me in these pale inconceivable suburbs?

Here they come, those enervating proles,
Impossibly tongue-tied: Amor and Psyche, bearing
Zinfandel. Hey, who's watching the kids?
They're so in love they just can't spare the time.

Quanta, galaxies—it's all God's brain;
And we're its ephemera, fancies; memories
Of futures past and bygone days to come.
Space-time curls at my feet, snug as a cat.

MY CENTURIES

Trakl perceived it. The visages, the healers,
innumerable vistas, arms, legs, balm.
"I'll try to induce His Excellency to appear.
                              What shall we say?
      Did you say something?"
                          I incline
To vertigo, myself.
        And you, Mabuse
                —did you say something?

The light crinkles over the rocks; the sails
Cascading over skyscrapers—
               Kolyma, Nagasaki, Heaven, Earth:
We look about, transfigured,
                    though nothing has changed.
Touch wood, and flounder in gravity and blood.

These Gesthemenic cities, groin girt high,
Horns, claws, and sackcloth. Now we start again;

New types press at the zeniths. Ah -- my centuries!

DRESDEN

I

Final scene. Askew metropoli.
The raining sylphs of death. The glacier stars,
Pale only. True removal.
What were their supplications,
Imploding to a destiny of insects?
That terror would spare them?
The noon of pain,
Mandragora-drunk,
Feed ever elsewhere?
Blindness of nations.

II

Impenitence
Unto this last.
The sirens fail,
All slantings cease,
The ceased or grey to endlessness begin.
A rustle as leaves coalesce. No use.
No end, no use, no salvage. Nothing more.
Folly, the breath of sessile day,
Stretches wide his wings of flame.
Embraces raze the river-grey

Malefic cities,
Onieric swagger
Of nerve and figure,
Ground and desire;
Collective imago
Unearthing the star Wormwood.

III

After true light
We roam the frost
The ashen hawks
Cry as the last
Occured despair,
To falconer come,
Shrivels there.
And then there were none.

Excremental night, welcome.
Welcome to the Machine.

ASCENDING STAIRS

Longevity. The world declines to shadow
Like morning into evening; or old slippers
Worn with decrepit shuffles, ankle-thorned,
Bearing an epoch's footfalls. So it goes;
The days successive day-dreams, and the rich
Heavenly banquet ever out of reach.

Yet rain will glaze an icéd leaf,
Becoming pure Idea; starlit corn
Patiently wait for summer; and the soul,
Virtuoso of fallenness, blink its eyes and waken,
Opening to God. This happens. Who knows why?
Despite ourselves we climb ascending stairs.

VALKYRIE

We rode, my Gods and I, through ash once cities.
We sang the wordless songs we sang before,
Fluttering like banners that are only mortal.

We circled them again, the endless fallen,
Who trail across the earth like windblown hair,
Whom we shall greet till time comes to an end.

Wolves sip the stream, curled eyes austere and bare,
As the blue river writhes beneath their stare.

I AM A BAT

After Kunert

I am a bat.
You do not hear,
Human, my shriek,
For human ears
Are not attuned
To its high tones;
But my brethren
In their bones
Feel it shiver
And respond
As it quivers
Far beyond
My black throat
And off the
Things around us
Showing me
All the world
My eyes would spy,
With its echo;
Thus we fly.

Off the treetop,
Barn and steeple,
The cave wall,
And the people,
Rings return
To serve as eye.

But when silenced,
Voiceless, we
Strike and shatter
As we bound;
On walls tattered;
Spinning down.
Pleasing some,
For our dark wings
Frightens those
Who fear such things.

But then the vermin
Whom we ate
Begin to
Proliferate;
And devour,
Where we but sang.

Human, you
Shall miss us then.

TRINITY

Outwards from Ground Point Zero fissures run;
Tar-knotted surfaces rake in monad flame;
Shards splintering out like millionfold swirls of wrens
Spiral in a manifested sun.
At the heart? There is no thing, no one;
Nor in the intermediate fused-glass breast.
Miles off, test dummies twirl and, swath for crest,
Men from enclosures take up Geiger aim
At warm obliteration from that pen
Where abstract and insensate furies nest
In wait, to unsheathe talons and to caw
Scatologies from the Atom's broken jaw
On continents and species soon but final
Red bits of meat for strontium hawks to maul.

COLLAGE OF BEAUTIFUL

Under the blazing sun on the beach at sunset
                                          it's always you,
And the sound of waves that quench my thirsty body.
Tomorrow, I'll let myself flow beyond the waves
As the sea breeze blows,
                      fashionable picture till the midnight.

Human beautiful life, colorful rainy days,
Let's make yeah proposal to sway of old.
Cinema of monochrome, let's feel the beat,
Go wild, heart on fire, and interface.

Super-hit me now! Imposition of night club,
Power of suit, latin chicka boom,
For that whole body thirst situation.
A contemporary urban wave of mandom
Catching no border. The human days

A happy present of the world.

THE FIGURE

It's never there when you look at it directly;
The figure running alongside you, skimming nigh
Like a coverlet of spiders, or the moth
That topples circling in the lit oil-lamp,
Completing the circle. Draw
Your automatic in one easy motion –
But it's too late. The face in the dark pool's
Swooned outward into yawning radii,
Sinking at last in glints, hobnail, and spittle.

Contrariwise, the girl on the far shore --
A bloom of reminiscent visages,
Anomalous and silent, hair adrift
In filaments like ensigns flax as coin --
Regards you with quiet solicitude,
Like a word from some long-erasèd mouth,
In calm and shining garments.
                              Ah, but by
Her side the figure thrusts its stumps at you.

SUSAN SONTAG (1933-2004)

The words decay, the words decay and fall
Like divers gawking at the curvatures
Of intrapsychic layers: wingéd crutch,
Which in the end exhausts, for are they not
Tautology? A Nietzchean affluence
Shrugs off such thin personae, mots de noir –
Asseverations ill as which may botch
Sole singulars into a parable
Whose maps revive hysteria's astrolabe;
As now slips tattered into what will be.

Europamüde, baby, then. Farewell.
When you returned from Paris it was cold.

COUNTENANCE

Whose hand, whose countenance? Our eyes are closed;
The universe no answer; netherworlds
Of the mundane our bestiary; yet
The skeins of song, unparalleled, sigh on,
Like eve, or specters, all dissolved in morning—
Far beacon swallowed up in arrogant light.

Dream and interpretation: smoke and glass
Exchanging glances. Press your knife to the
Heart of the portrait and the sitter dies,
Dorian-like; well-daubed solidity
A brinksmanship of ghosts. Yet who would feign
That face his own, or stay the pen that scrawled
This breviary that surrounds me now?
Knowing the *koiné* in its original language
Chastens one, as though a shadow trails you;
Knowing we do not know as we are known.

Our fate, our joy. Who dares pry them apart?
I pause before the cool ubiquitous frame.

COLD BOUNTY

The hawks' cold bounty. They remain, allure,
Endeavoring intensely. And the cities,
Full of such calm shadows as they eye
In towering certainty the silent evenings.
We were such soarings once, such shadows; like
The breathing birds now roaming.

Inevitably there were lesser moments.
Ones which fed
The pale stones rain,
Sit poised in the naked darkness each one shelters,
Policing the silent pavements of the heart,
Collective interior night,
Like a grazing of minnows fleeing in anxious thicket;
Fleeing from you as you have fled from others.

Let us lie quiet now, now in that winter,
                              quieter than a stare;
Hear the private streaming faces, round with sadness,
True to their treacheries. Tightly, the fragments burn
With a fury like the stars; once bright perhaps,
Now shut
Grey eyelids.

But there is more to you, as you environ
Their shimmering, their bountiful, torments.

UNAUSSPRECHLINGEN

Were we not all afraid of the city?
The hours of quarantine, the indistinct
Police, alluvial windows, boulevards
Of shuttered voices, flesh and spear and spire,
The very windows aviaries, fjords?
So many slump and rave against the walls,
Scalene shadows conjoined to their heels,
Unraveling the exquisite silk of time,
As blades of wings, near, fall, like guillotines:
Swans sculling on the rippling Muscat surface
Of the charred river.

World so askew;
The quiet wind, sigh-haired;
Tiger moths swirling in the dissecting room;
The wisps of dust, the flail of winter rains,
Streaking our irises like crack-streaked glass
Or an entangled spider. I
Remember...

                Sick palazzo. Rain.
Dusk cloven all around and
Slit thorax red and grinning
Under an ova of most immense sky.

21

Such animations in that smear of eve
Were sunlight: glints of near-Rilkean angels,
The rebus of their tesseract Bosch pinions
Thrumming out laggard beats mechanically
Atop the Trade Center where, gathered, they sang
Time-stunted carols of their solitude,
(Floodwaters soft withdrawing to the sea),
Their eyes a gnomon,
Final coda,
As it is in Heaven.

Or the charred river.

And you, my heir, the symbol;
Whose hollowed houri grieve,
Adrift among these gentle dead,
These dry absinthine leaves.

TWELVE LINES

Sometimes, elusive friend, I dream of hell;
Though it has passed, a residue remains;
Forfeitures of dearness, *lachrimae;*
Late holes of self where silence must collect.
These fearsome tapestries you slew with light,
As morning throws aside the shards of night.

Would that you dwelt in me as grace in you
Dwells gleaming, amethyst water of new life;
Bright sustenance, at whose melodious glance
Forgotten words revive -- Beauty, and Art --
My fellow casualties. Now they walk whole,
And shining as they take your equal hands.

BRIDAL

The celebrants submerged her hair in rosaries
As salamanders slid up, down, the stairs.
Her lambent gaze, her swaddled pause,
                              seemed cleansed,
Relieved of wondering if darkness was there.

Laughing twisting gasping she endured
The splintering 'mid her thighs. And, rudely hewn,
The ancient wetness ran down her pale legs.
Thundery rain of a summer afternoon.

In time the zoologic paunch conceived,
Darkening time's triumph. Fetal shrieks,
Muttering daggers in the viscera,
Fluttered to her ears from the bald peak

Shredding her cleft, like a stuck-out tongue.
And afterwards she was no longer young.

A FEW MOMENTS TO BREATHE

We took a few moments to breathe, but afterwards
Were made the sultans of the tribe. I judged
Our work complete. The final pacification
Of sundry primitives we left to arms
Whose searing swathes recalled Imperial days.

The brutes all round beat time with bone and brayed
Refrains at sunlight. Soon terrific gusts
Of scorching heat swirled, ominous, from the South.
Ill luck: a scorpion with a human face
Stung me severely as I lay to sleep.
And soon by day and even in the sunshine,
The sands of time grew curved and unnatural.

The paroxysm flourished; into black pools
Of horror soon I sank, unravelling;
Vast broods of Levianthic vultures, Christ-
Like in wing-span, yet not Christ, tore at
My eyes, my liver. Slurred subhuman voices
Incessant spread chimera crosswise changed
New fecal landscapes. Terrified, I prayed;
Dim lights sang cautions indecipherable.

Perforce the phantoms saddled up, slunk off,
Their tempers roughened by my freaks of mirth.
And as the sun climbed, so I shifted swiftly
To a pale cloak that filtered out its torrents.

I basked in that warmth, gazing across the dunes
At the towering spiders, philosophical and silver,
Their slim metallic tibia astride
The time-corrupted pyramids;
Who gleaming paused in contemplation; then
Turned starwards into new and undefined lands.

'LUCIFER, ABRUPT'

Lucifer, abrupt. His realm. Strange light
Shafts from the maimed scenes glittering at his back
Where his cool glassy and quite blood-stained hands
Thrust the great edifying dead. Acquaintance, glance:
Old worms and larvae of Hell's underskin:
Centurions, slaves, pope-kings, courtiers,
Heretics, child-whores. Defunct as dung.
Rare purport sears us, where such struck extrude
Minutiae of torment, panoply
Of spleen, high anguish, expenditure of hissings;
Classic tableaux observed. Our eyes
Ransack their anti-ecstacies for gist
Opaque to contemporaries. Be it so.
What adamantine strewn. What progeny.

CATASTROPHE

So pale; she loved you; hard to believe.
Where is she gone? No stir, no sound,
Here at the end, eyes shut, no sign,
In no time gone and in the ground.

Little to tell, far less to say.
Long night takes longing day away.
No getting out. No going on.
Ah the truth begins to dawn.

Quiet the winterchill on the breeze.
Quiet the seraphs, stone the child.
Catastrophe, how, why, like that?
Son of man, another time.

THE EXTERMINATOR

From the memories of my childhood I could deduce
The mimes of fascism, the secret of the Gospels;
That its brightest rooms
               were the private domains of police
          Extrapolating crippling provisos;
Sadisms of immemorial schemata.

So—may I be so bold?—philosophy
Is simply a poorly executed portrait.
Let no mask speak to you, for you too are
Disfigured beyond recourse and do not know it.
Shush as the gods pick up their knives and forks.
These bleating New Men know
Whom they do and do not intend to murder.
Hitler, old drummer boy, be still a moment.
Calmly, unerringly, the ship goes on its way.

THERE

Ten thousand years and what will be left?
Shadows falling across the sands.
Dead leaves fluttering across the shadows.
I rise from them, I join them once again.

Ground Zero, planes roar, the radioactive girl
Waves to you to join her on the platform,
Her folded wings reflecting
The galaxies, the universe.
Go on. Why not? You're already there.

White sails where the present century collapses.
Chernobyl, Coca-Cola, Sailor Saturn.
Birds swirl up from winter trees.
I'm shaking, old friend,
Shaking with laughter.

THE ABSTRACTED MAN

As pigeons feasted off the excrement
Of horses outside, he walked down slanting stairs,
Past the girls in their tinsel skin below
Petting machine-pistols, and said hello.

The autumn evening bent the high green stars
To wan and papal marks, hovering cruci,
Under which the abstracted man now rushed,
His groin all clock-faces, his quick eyes hushed.

And, the next day, capitulating to nightmare,
As he removed his face out of respect
For the body of a murdered schoolgirl,
Her stare became somehow more tolerable;

And strewn along all the halls, all along the corridors,
The snarl of the world began another journey.

ASHEN DAY

Shall I never see the sky?
Till your echo dies away,
Whiteness all unbroken still,
Where the evening murmurs; then,
As your lovely shadow strays
Halfway to the fancied dead,
Shall it fly my memory
And leave me the ashen day.

As above, thus so below,
You who were my special joy:
Flowers fall as time descends
And becomes eternity.

KEK JOKING

1

Angels pull back the curtains round a bed
To look down on the faces of the dead,
Until the dead are absent altogether.
Such fragments of Gothic utterance cling to us;
A last grey bread of degradation.
When that we find our pinions furled and coiled,
The sooner we are rid the better
Of our sarcophagi, whether vice or virtue.
Humiliator, avenger; despoiler, redeemer --
The basis of the ashes shields its slurs;
And the name's womb is covered in lament.
But is such consequence remarkable?
The refuse of one world is embryo
To another, for all images of life
Are rooted in either swaddling cloth or shroud.

2

Uncover my face; mine eyes dazzle; I died young.
"Are you really 111 years old, Miss?"
They pulled the implant plug out of my neck
And set a net and waited. My ghost dove,
Playing the invariable game. 12 rounds 6 seconds
Into a human silhouette: AI signals
Were traced to the models with oldtype genomes --
The infiltrators. "Buy or die," they say.
All information that is spread is real,
Internally structured, all in one fell swoop;
Software erasure of a software dream,
That is all. And as I quickly reloaded
In the Jardin des Plantes, a puppet shed her clothes.

"Kek," she said, intensely, "does not joke."

DARE

How shall I ever dare
To look you in the eye
And confess you are
The rose within my heart,
A fever in my soul,
And all my thoughts' delight?

I have no power to leave;
Lest one of your dear hands
May some day gesture, 'Stay,'
And bind me with a band
I cannot flee: your face,
Eyes glittering as stars.

'Beloved creature, dare:
The adolescent day
Must pass, and if you share
This last dream of my heart
Till awful evening break,
No sorrow would I give but only grace' -

But that I cannot say,
For evening draws too near;
So let my actions speak
With graciousness more clear,
Fulfilling all you seek;
More loving than words may.

EXTINGUISHED

The child, the Shining Ones said, learned and learned
How Being ebbed through long invasive time;
How stars would crumple in their terminal bourns;
How light slunk mindlessly; the paradigm
That garlands neither manifest nor stay,
Despite Good's quite articulate dismay.

Mysterious to us as null to God,
The great perplexity Himself was stumped
As wounds and fissures waltzed across the sod,
Ring-around-rosy round the tot now slumped.

What *was* what was extinguished, the child asked?
And the long winter faltered like a mask.

GOSSAMER REDCURRANT

Ventricles in talons' pare and beak:
Staatspolizei in all their ebony,
Dissecting lustrous shadows. Hear the shrieks?
The sums and siphons of my century?

> *The bullet struck her head;*
> *Gossamer redcurrant.*
> *The bayonet his back;*
> *Alizarin jam.*
> *The saw hacked off her breast;*
> *Magenta gelatins.*
> *Where shall we three meet again?*
> *Cherries of marzipan.*

A crumpled wick, a house of cards, a press
Of breast on furtive breast, the siren rain:
We entertained the particulars of darkness,
Our Braille discourse so murderous and vain.

> *The bombs tore off their legs;*
> *Cinnabar burgundies.*
> *The torches lit their hair;*
> *Raspberry sweet jelly.*
> *Bright atoms spilt their eyes;*
> *Heliotrope blancmange.*
> *In thunder, lightning, or in rain:*
> *Apples of marzipan.*

'Where were you, O insolvent Paladin?'
Melodious silences murmur in each case.
It's your only chance. As *Existenz*
Takes out its pistol; aims it at your face.

CONSUMMATION

You are mistaken. No one was unkind.
But seeing me there among the shadows, fading,
Slovenly and unassimilable, surely
My end and my beginning proved the same.

The bleatings drew a crowd where it was done;
A flurry of eyes that slithered to attention;
Dust and flies. I was not violent as
The apertures to elsewhen slowly shut.

No say in the matter. Why, then, was there ease,
Raising my writhing face towards horizons
Like a caressing voice, a secret passage?

Who said, with happy melancholy, 'Shall
You spend some time among us, visitor?'
As, silence gouging me, I fell away.

FAR FROM ME

At touch of sun the evening's grays unfurl,
Majestic, ambidextrous. How like you --
Familiar alm, so suddenly ray-streaked;
Annunciation; darkness overthrown;
A swoon of birds from branches. Yes, I know:
Intoxication is a poor way to love.
Yet round you, star-like, flickering, I so turn:
Your dazzled moth, autumnal with withinness.

Outside, the world of data, coin, and steel
Crackles and executes its hiss of shadows;
Day's urgent ciphers writhe with craft and self,
Flesh locks, time's roseate mandalas beckon.
And where you are not of it? There is nothing.

Yet you are not far from me. I look round,
Unknowing where to turn, yet you are here,
Dear in grace and presence,
Puzzled as I am at my baffled love.
Quite unaware that in
Your hand the slender rose of heaven opens.

DOWNFALL

Crematoria had ceased to matter,
Like the foul smell. Who had the right to judge?
Our evenings turned instead to masterworks
Obsequious to man, not to the bounds
Of the expressible. The camps, the war,
Were neither extremity nor passion, for
On its ragged hook upon a wall,
The body claims that true simplicity
Which no more seeks and so cannot be found.
Yet on the stains that steal
Throughout that world were carven harshnesses
As luminous as painful, and
The calls and murmurs of an endless shore,
Whose architectures weal the grain of time,
Were nowise diminution. I and thou:
I place these two against that same bright ground.

METROPOLI

I search my books and papers, gather disciples.
When offers come, I seriously consider them.
The antidepressants are therapeutic, and my cock
Has a hidden significance.
Gently I dip my toe in Wittgenstein's blood,
Trying not to slip, metropoli
Glimmering in the gently drowning distance
As the impossible staff move into place
Waiting for the order to fire.

Was there another way? Or did it only
Seem as though confrontation, passionate,
Incivil, necessitated my fall?
All I know is, it was winter then,
Hammerklaviers ringing like a thousand Dantons,
In the town square, by the Presbyterian Church,
Exposing the secret illnesses of the gods.

AN ARC OF TIME

You glide as though across a frozen lake—
To where? No one is there left to remember.
Look at the time. So late, my dear, so late;
October winter glistens in the rain.

Faraway points of light blink in the darkness
Like faces of passengers huddling at the platform
For the last train, or aged communicants.
Clouds drift slowly past and then break up.

Was it for this that you were born, this place,
This hour, this intersection? High, a bird,
Neither exultant nor decipherable,
Transects the sky along an arc of time,
Skirting the glittering tips of wildwood ranges.

OPHELIA'S SCISSORS

Deuteronomy of vellum, tilting floors
That kiss away all Stygian emphasis;
Free-falls of whorish squares and fecund sprites:
Blind glance that flowers at the speed of night.

We must endure the ground rules. Honeysuckle's
Warm crowns wind-whispering curt terminus.
The star-beasts wheeling, glazing, past our heads.
Schlafe, mein kind, mein kind: the huge dull wound.

Out of the augurs, running from my room,
I woke in the astonishing light of birds
Cawing cloaca – our hid time-torn selves –
With the perfect insincerity of scissors.

Ubique: grey flowers in grey vases.
Ophelia cuts the sun and moon in slices.
'Come: I hover grinning in dark space,
Preserved in amber. Come,' she says, 'your grace.'

GENUG

We lose all we possess -
The currents of the spring,
The restless welts of time
That flicker in serene
Oblivious ambience.
What breath of it is not
Illusory at last,
Nor in the closure null?
Come, shadow; take my hand.

MATERIAL FOR YOUR ART

Sink your teeth into my heart:
It is material for your Art.
All my pain and grief and pallor
Pen and ink shall line and color.
Into tatters am I torn?
Scratch them down as line and form,
As you shape each welt and sear
Into shade and cross-hatch, dear.
One who is an artist truly
Must portray one's subjects coolly;
If they bleed, well, what of it?
Ruby reds are exquisite
And tears as blue as amethyst—
So give the knife an extra twist.
For the amusement of your friends,
Turn my wounds that sere and rend
Into pencilled line. Your name
May gather critical acclaim.

SHADOWFALL

Unrequited shadowfall
Calls to ashes all in all.
Time in time shall all things sever.
In my arms, beloved, gather:

May clandestine evening eye
Our brief day here tenderly;
And recall our hours, our laughter,
Till God's morning come thereafter.

Though forgotten evils wither
Words unspoken ache forever.
Know I loved you in full measure;
You, who were my life's one treasure.

REKI

Long pale have I perceived you, which were flesh;
In winter now as white as childhood.

This sign the elaborate language, cynosure:
This tiny breach of ash. O skein of screens,

Judge my lost life. My flights. The pyrrhic silence;
Late, oaken, stalagmitic; tor of rust

Scarved in plurality of shadows,
Querulous and tattered. Lunar place.

But in lascivious winter still you dress,
Sere and relinquished, as the heaven-born go,

Crying presence where the whorl of lies proceeds,
Inordinate, pale and severed. Crying. Keening.

SERPENTS OF HISTORY

Ice-bitten, I recall
The Russian word for snow,
Red kerchiefs, Komsomol,
The scarlet rockets' glow.

Cut-blazoned, I call out:
Steppe-horsemen long departed,
What blank fate led me here,
So severed and distorted.

How is it that I came to be
Shipwrecked, though neither ship nor shore
Bore me, nor winds, nor bearing sea,
So far, so infinitely far,

My shipmates drowned in seas of time,
Its scarlet depths and lees;
The teeth around them the green Rhine-
Serpent's of History.

RED CITIES

The olden things, the cacodemons, boded
Ill as lost bodies roamed the intervals;
The light; its dimness. And of course the war—
That war now over many years ago.

Little by little history takes form
And is forgotten, done to death, *kaput*;
The ruins-strewn inner landscapes no more ours;
The new things we achieve, the very air.

But under the blows of that transition, voices
Suffocate within us, die like clouds
(Those forests of greatcoats waiting to be shot)
Devoid of recollection. Vehement

Red cities, patience in your brief surcease.
Calmly futurity sows the wind, the breeze.

LES ENFANTS DU PARADIS

A comedy in seven movements

I

The Triumph Of Love

James Joyce had twenty-five operations on his eyes. Sigmund Freud had thirty-three operations for cancer of the mouth and throat. Wystan Hugh Auden was arrested for urinating in Barcelona. Sir Winston Churchill was an anti-semite.

II

Deep Blue: White Pawn To Bishop Four

'I do not want to be I, I want to be We!'
Bakunin said that. (Much despised by Marx.)
A large hill of a man, hirsute, slope-shouldered;
No Tsarist.

> In the whorehouse of the mind:
> That's where you define 'define'.
> A swirl of crows, an odor of sperm:
> *Place de la Révolution!*

> Witchcraft of princes at the Dresden Gates.
> Apples and a noblewoman
> In a snow-white landscape.

>> Sing it, Ozzy:

>>> *Checkpoint Charlie*
>>> *falling down*
>>> *falling down*
>>> *falling down*

Checkpoint Charlie
falling down

Vy Vyezhayetye Iz Amerikanskogo Sektora
Vous Sortez Du Secteur Americain
Sie Verlassen Den Amerikanischen Sektor
You Are Now Leaving The American Sector

Bye!

III

Neural Slice

This sentence is a lie.

Man is a dog with a brain;
His leash, gold's horrible grin;
His bone, war's scarlet plain;
His bitch: evolution.

Multimedia now embrace
Der Hund in every human face:
D'avignon, no Attic posture;
Transience, not alabaster.

Deliberate regression. *Zerfall.* Yet
Amid the tall green stalks, amid the corn—
Angels singing.
A blaze of blossoms.
Veritatis splendor.

Scenting perished stars,
Time's wolves break through the gate;
A mysticism for beginners—
Darling, don't be late!

    Nietzche in Turin. See, it starts to snow.

IV

We Are Borg

Zauberflšte, Zauberberg
Resistance is futile.
Resistance is futile.

Gomen na sunao ja nakute
You will be assimilated.
You will be assimilated.

Napolean had hemorrhoids
Karl Marx had them too.
As did Wordsworth. Very sad.
Pu wee tu wit a woo.

As amid blotches of furniture,
God sat silent as Heidegger,
Eyeless in Gaza at the techno raves.

March, hare!

Television Commentator A: 'Since we're changing we must be improving!'

Television Commentator B: 'Since we're moving we must be getting closer!'

There were seas and mountains
Sharp dorsal fins
Membranes primeval
Genescapes of kins

Prayers like knives
Towers gull-swirled
Engravings of Hokkaido
Abysses of pearl.

I want to go to Heaven.

V

The Interpretation Of Dreams

Eliot was an anti-Semite;
Schopenhauer was one too;
Richard Strauss and Richard Wagner,
Santayana, Diderot,

Henry Ford, Mohammed also,
Juvenal, Roy Campbell, Kant,
H.L. Mencken, Seneca,
Celine, and Henri Montherlant;

Schwarzkopf, Flagstad, Paul de Man,
Hemingway and Wyndham Lewis,
Jonathan Edwards, André Gide,
St. Ambrose (and Lindburgh too was)

Shaw, Aquinas, Whistler, Chekhov,
Philip Larkin, 'Chinese' Gordon,
Arnold Toynbee, Pound, Karl Barth,
William Shakespeare, Chaucer, Wharton;

Henry James, Mussorgsky, Fichte,
Henry Adams, Gottfried Benn,
St. Jerome and St. Augustine,
Tacitus, Quintilian;

Queen Victoria and Treischke,
Dreiser, Pushkin, Robert Lowell,
e.e. cummmings, Bismarck, Belloc,
H.G. Wells and Roald Dahl;

Marcion and Simone Weil,
Heidegger; Drieu La Rochelle,
Leni Reifenstahl and Luther,
Jean Cocteau; Colette as well;

Julian Assange, Walt Disney,
Dr. Seuss, Coco Chanel;
Winston Churchill, Solzhenitsyn,
Diderot, Drumont, Ravel.

Weininger, Schmitt, Andrew Anglin,
Bobby Fischer, Jung and Belov,
Orwell, Calvin, al-Farabi,
Paul, Peter and Piuses I through XII.

Dostoyevsky, Wolfe, Erasmus,
Ramses, St. John, Gyp, Ernst Rohm,
Igor Stravinsky and Knut Hamsun,
Dickens, Degrelle, Degas.

                    Shalom.

VI

The Battle Of Borodino

Homo futurus: man is now no more.
Ice-ages beckoning; polar debris.
We ran, we ran, choking in thickets of time;
Sleipner pawing air, and whinnying in north light.

-- Beam us up, Scotty.

> Off the bottle,
> On the rocks,
> We writhe like
> Medusa's locks.
>
> Kirin, strychnine,
> Tsing Tao too,
> Playboy Bunnies,
> We love you.
>
> This sentence is a lie.

VII

Laika

Josef Vissarionovich Dzhugashvili, a cobbler's son and former seminarian, was an anti-semite. Late in life he authored a celebrated monograph on linguistics.

In August 1949, the first Soviet thermonuclear device was detonated in the northeast Kazakhtan region of Semipalatinsk.

In November 1957, the first living terrestial mammal -- the dog Laika -- was successfully launched into space.

In April 1961, Yuri Alekseyevich Gagarin's Vostok spacecraft completed an orbit of the Earth.

In March 1953, Josef Vissarionovich Dzhugashvili died of a stroke in his rooms at Kuntsevo as a performance of Wolfgang Amadeus Mozart's 23rd Piano Concerto played quietly beside him.

> *Moskva moya!*
> *Drazha moya!*
> *Ty Samoya*
> *lyubov moya!*

Exeunt.

The Age of Steel

ARCHAIC SONNET

I drown in eyes as though in sunlit streams;
At swirls of hair I slow and dissipate;
I dream of arms that are not arms but dreams;
I drown in chasm eyes. Yet, in such state,
Dark wakefulness disturbs me. Do I err?
Do even such eyes deserve such reverence?
Or does my trance ridiculously bare
Desire's ego, aching and intense?
But then you pass; I drink your perfect sheen;
And feel no stain, nor hear the soul's base wolves;
I see your lips part, trace your hand, and in
That grace, my doubt and O my heart dissolves.
Wherefore my mind, to your dear sweetness bound,
    Turns round,
        turns round,
            turns round,
                turns round,
                    turns round.

Rudi Matić

CRUDE SPADE FACE

Antennae of appalling grace
Probe my weary crude spade face,
And my aural lily bones
Terminate like eels like norns
Like pharmaceuticals. They wax
Bright as bright *grand mal* attacks,
Ripcord jubilant, gold as snow --
This all nibelungen know.
Quartered in such terminal quarters,
Lot's prehensile bruised nude daughters'
Pointillistic Blood Type (O)
Was washed clean long years ago.
On their hands graze your eyelashes;
Anteaters rampage through the ashes.

RAINY DAY

I must change my life?
Maybe tomorrow.
Today the rain is falling
Like footsteps on the moon,
Or the shadow of a Zeppelin
Drifting wordlessly seawards,
Folding my wounds
Into an origami.

Shutting my eyes I see
The multifoliate things:
The poignant stones
The shadowy mountains
Old shoes
An unread Simenon
The unfurling sail
The birdsong in the garden
This cup of coffee, hot and black
Science fiction
Donald Trump

How did it come about
That I am here?
And where *is* this, exactly?

                        Emptiness,

Open the door.
It's gotten stuffy.
            Sure,
The days trail downwind
                      after one another;
Like smoke
        the birds trail softly down the sky;
Behind the clouds
                the moon breaks like a fart.
So what?

        There is no need to leave this world.

AUTUMNAL

The gods of man: the crack in the facade.
That morning of tomorrows fell away.
But orders have been given, paeans bleat.
The void remains discernible enough.

No words. No ceremony. I set sail.
New permutations gather, old assume
The camouflage of days, withdrawn yet not;
Earth, fire, water, air, I slip away,
Winding, a slow and languorous cortège,
Against the cramped horizons—
Wolf Man: autumnal, liminal, assured:
Discarding the continua of farewells;
Embracing vacuity;
Guttering to ash in Cheshire grins of time.

What shadows fall between us and the world!
The enigmatic gulls that, like ourselves,
Are sick of man. After victory, brightness?
So we thought. Not so.

The sea of words will ache forever.
Sail homeward, wakening from everything.

VICTORIANA AUTUMN

Consummate summer falters: one by one,
The cooled cranes spiral from this shut of sun.
Lilac collapses where toothed breezes feed;
Once blood-burst leaves contract to flake and screed.
The warm grain-fields that tolled their
                                      brass-bronze tinge
Pass mortal to shorn stick and silvered fringe.
The lambent gnats that sang in azure massings
Chill air dissolves; smooth argent gilds their passings.
Cinnamon noon expires in amber bands;
Its twilit after, under aspic wands.
The sick West sires snow to numb the sense;
Moth time disfeatures the exhausted dance.
And from her exile in a lunar pearl,
Incredibly slides night to still and furl.

TRAWLING THE ABSOLUTE

Trawling the Absolute, we dredge
Singsong and nullity, rodomontade,
Up that shore's diurnal edge.
Von Paulus at Stalingrad

Had no such luxury, nor Joan
Of Arc, rope-tied and faggots blazing,
As the Absolute forced the door
And existence burst sans reason.

An aerie above poetry:
That's what I sometimes must envision:
Gangrenous intellection scorned;
An immaculate derision.

A WHITENESS

As sibilant as snow, that awfulness:
The light of Heaven on the weight of Earth;
Consummate, absent, call it what you will,
It does not waver, bend, but only stream
Endless assent, in möbii of ribands
That inlay beauty on all that they have
Predestined us to love, and we are lost,
Ever to mark those plays of passing light.

Under the name of God, under its sword,
Under the shoals of late pale fallen snow,
Under the penitence of shadowy walls
Whose every stone is spectral, under boughs
Where there is no deception, lies a whiteness:
Time's limitless forehead, stung. The prick of thorns.

WHAT WE DID

We spoke of children regularly shot
In occupied territories; of the old
Clapped into shabby nursing homes to rot;
Of how the Afghan winters are quite cold.

We talked of rife metastasizing AIDS
Sprawling like foliage; of clitoral
Excisions in the sub-Saharan glades;
Of gill-armed headless tots by Chernobyl.

We said it really was a lousy thing
That Tienanmen's Chinese were still in cells;
That Pol Pot died in bed; that there were rings
Of wire, barbed, round Palestinian hills.

We said things just could not go on this way.
And what we did was have some more pâté.

THE COMING STORM

"Roman hardness. Soon there will be no room
for anything else." Perhaps. No inwardness,
that inner flight of cranes, but only
the Faustian outline visible, sans ambivalence.
For the first time we recognize ourselves –
Lascivious shiver.

Coldness is not such a bad thing. *Je suis mystique*.
Here, gods, you dazzling bastards – taste it: blood!
Bouquet of Brobdingnag and marzipan.

Vulnerant omnes: ash, a wind of knives,
Will represent mankind before the gods;
and nothing else will be of consequence.

IN THE ALBERS ROOM

Irrelevant the stars
Seem, in quark decay;
Lower entities take on
Through the concrete day

Thick engulfing bulk:
The job, the bills, one's gut:
The reproductive slaver:
The civic jackboot. But

Those stellar shadows' brittle
Mnemonic aftertaste
Limns the mental palate,
However swift our haste

Or great our depredations
In the stifling day,
Murmuring a knowledge:
Star matter is our prey,

Or we are its. A conflict
Millenia shall seal;
And human talons master
And fashion under heel.

DISPLACEMENTS

The invaders hovered above the androgynous cities,
Burning mid clouds. Birds started up from wires
In flocks, revolving, past the encircled species,
The obliterated squares. But in the next episode

There were roses in the vases and, beyond,
Were other landscapes, where kind farm girls feed
The lambs red apples. Virtual theatres, where
A pose of words conceals a mask of deeds.

What if tomorrow you should chance to scry
Iconic elegance? That stillness you
Misplaced? And everything you lost, returned?
Fording the river, what have we but these?

RAVENS FLOCK

The civic order rots to farce.
The papers hum with feral hate.
The spilling bombs from bombers course.
The bestial to the bestial prate

The paralytic common view:
'There is nothing to be done' --
'There is nothing I can do' --
As the victims burn and run.

Ravens flock to city walls
With their cool and Roman gaze
And a darkness that appals
As below we thread the maze

Of the pathways that we took:
Reason fled, ideals betrayed,
Money über alles. *Look:*
Do not turn your eyes away.

THE STARS FOR A WHILE STOPPED SHINING

The stars for a while stopped shining
Over the earlier, sunset-honeyed, trees.
But whispering within my ribcage, softly,
Calling like bells, that lambent light returned.

I was the empty street, the drugstore window,
The traffic light, high, waving in slow wind,
As time sang, changing, gazing out to sea,
Moving along the days, invisible.

Deepening into shadow. Soft, serene.
Like lifting birds who, though all flown away,
Return in season, as the darkness heartens,
The wheel stops slowly; twilight murmers. Yes,

It's evening now; the shops are closing, time
To go. Come back next day. Good night, good night.
The shades are drawn, the tailor's dummy mute
There in the window standing watch, the carousel

Sits quiet in the park across the way,
And tomorrow at the church bazaar,
A discount on Eternity, and tea;
Half off all used and reconditioned Gods.

THE HANDS OF HEAVEN

The stillness of the deep,
The plumage high above,
The star-sapphire buds,
The shining streams that rove
Beside the blossom-banks,
The hands of heaven close.

The hands of heaven reap
The feast of earth and shore,
The days that lose their light,
The hours that were fair
As birds that slowly sail
Away and are no more.

SLAPSTICK NOTHINGNESS

The Anti-instant is not so complex.
It is the spine of our contingency:
Damped gesture, extreme winterscape, the flea
Of the null; its zones swell and annex
Prolix experience, Kraken form, elude
Reconnaissance of language. 'Spirit'? 'Mind'?
The concepts vanish as they are defined.
We *sense* the marksman of our finitude;
And chafe in the bands of that experience.
Arabesques of the sterile seem a net:
To twist like hawks 'mid gutted Absolutes.
But the inevitable instant that uproots
The structure of all instants mocks such bents;
Seizures of slapstick nothingness rear and jet.

HOW THIS SADNESS CAME
TO BE PERSISTENT

The traceries were often beautiful.
But rendered on the Gnostic frieze they bore
Annihilated circumambulations,
Deliberate treacheries; from which stone of shore

The face of a wall soared up; up, infinite --
Signing the thicket signature of time,
Whose finger is a fire and whose eye
Proved serpentine as arrows.
                                    That is when
The heaps of stones collected into cities;
Why the confessors and the hangmen faltered;
How this sadness came to be persistent.

Listen. The siren-calls. The thorns, the root:
Whose pale eviscerations since the Gothic
Well overawe a flesh now turned to splinters
Devoid of heldentenors;
Asymmetries of angels;
A falsity of waters
For which no one dare answer.

And on the eve a thunder stammers slowly;
And round the tall cool marble Nike shimmers
Chryselephantine darkness;
Scar of logos.

Rudi Matić

IMPERIUM

How far the reaches
Of the lands.
How high the dog star
Blue with cold.
How dry the leaves
Deciduous
Go back to dust.
How old, how old.

The four winds drowse.
The doldrums spread.
Dust-motes fall.
Rainfalls end.
Soldiers, arms,
Groan into mud,
Wordless. *Omnes
Exeunt.*

FIGURES ATOP THE REICHSTAG

They are not artless, though all stone is blind.
The forms of intellect and of mere sensation
Diverge, foretokening the rend of tendons
Constraining them. Particular evidence:
Hooves loosed against the ripples of the clouds
As though disdaining mortal earth to trod on;
The plumes of wings set sovereignly in their places;
Each face, upturned to light, is shadowless,
Insensible, where time has found its halt.

Savagery too is meant to be conclusive.
Traveler, if fate has called you, answer.
Here is a fasting figure, skin and bone.
Here is your spade: dig now.

NO EXIT

God, departing shadow, turn. We have
Travelled so far together—plaited thorns.
Dust settles in the darkness; we confess;
The dead fly past; You've seen it all before.

We bear the double handicap of time,
Gather the sheltering Kafkan harvest. Like
Bats, the wind cries under our lapels,
Out of our burning eyes, our burning hair.

Too late now; too late, too late, too late.
The pornotopia implodes. After all these
Interrogations of nothingness, what confession?
Light, scan the silence of an unread page.

STARE

Watching the primordial outgoing tide,
The big loss no one ever talks about,
Crows sank into a moan of years of sunlight –
As, finally, something besides isolation happened:

Unraveling the world's pornographies,
Gorgeous confessors slowly knifed a girl
Along the sands astride the shoreless sea,
Like children in black blinding arriving roses.

Observing her duties in the impeccable war
Against the self, crows vomited bits of brain,
While the great crowd, and you yourself, applauded;
While crisply uniformed gods hovered in formation,

Their secret voices golden, dreaming new questions;
The wet red act now beveled by dazzles of sky.

THE INNER LIFE

What if the inner life has, after all,
No real existence?

Over Earl Grey I wonder now and then
At the awkward cable cars, the omnipotent police,
The soaring toll of discreetly sexual structures
That do not lack for clocks. Are they not calm
As cats preening their feathers, as the bells
Stinging the cold forever-April air,
Scattering that deafening radio silence?

                              Christian shades,
This posits Utopia reconciled at length
With our prosthetic face, don't you agree?
Salvation too presumes a garden where
No objects bulge or bump or overthrow,
Girth and dearth exquisitely marketed
—To a captive audience.

                              Who really is man?
The most significant questions are the ones
We can never answer.

A stray crow flaps down onto a streetlamp.

THE LONG MIGRATION

Extinction at the end of the Cretaceous.
Biological winter. Seas and wood perdure,
Severe and stark. The protohuman dawn.

What pseudomorphs glissade deep underneath
The surface of the amniotic water
We have grown old in drinking?

Ancestral roots dissemble. Over time,
The faces we construct to interact
Delusion makes our own.

Only am I myself against
Algol, Andromeda: far, indifferent, mute.
The cold intolerable Absolute.

THE PANTOMIME ERODES

The pantomime erodes. One's furtive hands,
Insentient shards, struck off sans bagatelle
Or mercies; furious abstractions, riven
Apart like half-lives or a slithering heaven.

You, this sonnet's protagonist, cannot
Hesitate. Like its meaning, you are not;
Unless each act is bullet-taut and pure,
Though frost slay the predestined falconer.

Glose cross-hairs now expose your pale girl-breast,
Illusory blackamoor: *Das Man, Das Ich,*
The scrotum winter, *allein,* aortal sighs;
The Last Men gathering like butterflies.

No renascence. No chalice. Plateux traced
Only at hawk extremes no mask dare face.

COLLECTED SILENCES

"Stillborn, the collected silences cry out:
Suddenly they are upon us, daggered shards,
Smelted in a metamorphosis of augurs.
Fantomas. Samsa. Ingsoc. Seigfried. Light?
O furtive heldentenor, in whose sight?
Ice-world, my insatiable pantomime, you begged
White light, convinced *you* were the protagonist.
Another error. Look at us, Queen of Heaven!
Our gestures like unfeathered arrows riven;
Blackamoor musculature scratching graffiti,
A heteroglossia of winter frost.
Here nothing is, nor ever was,
Save animated Fortinbras:
Card Captor, with thine aching lust,
Redeem us through thy sacral, ah! smooth breast."

I said. And then took out my stopwatch and clicked it,
Over a cup of tea with other duelists,
Awaiting a letter from the End of the World.

WAR IN THE AGE OF INTELLIGENT MACHINES

Sprawl of automata, bereft of tongue;
All that we see will surely disappear
In winterfall, slung wholly in that silence;
A lid of moths and after-wings. *Endlösung*,
Somnambulant ambience of close of day;
Whose nearness soon is neither frontispiece
Nor immanence, but sleep more cool than air,
Where all the tasks of flesh are obsolete.

Initialize.
Process.
Calculate.
Execute.

Ganglia rise in thermonuclear colors.
The earth the sea the cities shine like fire.
I press my fingers to the quiet stars.
War in the age of intelligent machines.

MY HUMAN FORM

Within the human day I wove
Mythologies of war and love
And fed my eyes on all that seems,
To gild my shred of time with dreams.

But time and day and all their lies
Proved shadows only children prize.
I tired of the shadows' storm.
And so I shed my human form.

Akin to eagles on the wind
I now roam past this mortal ken
Into the lands you do not know,
And keep no name nor feature more.

ZERO POINT

Precipices: incisor of a whore;
A sustenance of insects; monochrome
Flesh become rag, raped scrap torn off and flung;
This iron age of matter, slaver, bone.

It is impossible to express to you
How the four walls around me twist and scream;
As if they sensed a sea nearby, the ardor
God's transversal, silent, tigers scheme.

But that is the zero point we have not reached;
World as extrapolation of the talon,
Rather; portion fastened to we sad
Towering homunculi, adrift like pollen

Round it, turning circles, once, twice, thrice,
Vertiginously in this smite of ice.

ONE DAY

Extraordinary is the grace
Time brings to an aged face
Once belovéd, and now gone.
Sans its trace, one moves among
Bare hours as though through a waste:
For absent limbs do not embrace;
Nor ears hear absent words; nor eyes
Meet absent eyes; nor exile days
Recover their once-pleasant taste—
What gave them light has been erased.
Shall the sundered time that rends
The heart, come never to an end?
Dear one, cast to distant shores,
Shall both halves not meet once more?
The sun must rise again, again
The stars revolve, the seasons turn,
The clock-arms glide to where they were;
May it not also be so here?
All one can do is wait, and pray.
Dear friend, God grant one day that day.

OSTSEKTOR
in memory of
Friedrich Percyval Reck-Malleczewan (1884-1944)

I

The Duellists

In the sunlit garden
Hand in hand we promised
We would never
Fall in love.

In the high-domed greenhouse
We spoke as you were watering;
The ailanthus green
Beneath your touch.

At times we lay underneath the sheltering trees,
Or ran through rain like rose petals whirling in storms;
And sometimes we would sit by one another,
Beside the high ascending lancet windows.
At the ebony piano,
The Academy, *sehr Reichslich*, porcelain,
Silent, the corridors empty;
My fingers at a bagatelle, and you
Would sing, would sing, serene –

It was a bright cold day in April
And the clocks were striking thirteen.

>Do not enquire of a political prisoner
>Dirked frozen on scratches of barbed wire, gnarled
>Beneath a moon-lit opulence of snowflakes,
>The moral context or its extreme ground.
>Such dead assert a gangling independence
>From mortal hermeneutic. Far more steeled:
>Wind swirling in its polar grooves, resplendent.
>Before man, and after:
>The arctic horizon,
>Starlit parousia,
>Explicable falconer,
>Slaver and circlings,
>The arc closing, closing,
>Flickering swarming,
>The beaks and the claws,
>Even those circles ending
>Where I must end too;
>For the human will will not submit to you.

>>*Weisst du denn nicht, wem nur allein*
>>*Das Gold zu schmieden verginnt*

I shivered as you sang those passages
                            A music like the roses
        That grow at the end of the world.

And the butterflies, fluttering, shimmering,
                        The pinwheel swirling, I

Had to close my eyes.
                       You–was it you?–
    Touched my hair.

Birds in the sky.
Dust motes in the air.

    Vulnerant omnes. One of them shall kill.
    About my boots crawled parasitic entrails
    As masking chatter left its smoky mark,
    Smearing a numbness like a paradigm–
    New variations in syntactic chatter
    That did not matter.
    Each pose the Zeitgeist bid us ape
    Bore the implications of its rape
    Towards quite new solutions to the self:
    Metal fragments
    Falling,
    Falling,
    A vertiginous new donning,
    Towers taking wing.
    Storms of steel.
    Rains acetylene.

II

Heilige Nacht

I survived. By chance.
Spared pogrom teeth, the bombsight's glance,
I lived.
I should have liked to give
Some benediction; stoic utterance.
But I only mutter;
Gibbering old man—
Diaspora, no more centurion.

Carcinogenic Volga filled our boots.
Warmth paused, and all the Sol-vacated brunt
Concussed the world to leave vast pale dunes where
Laterals and diagonals tagged and waltzed
Pointillist splash and rampage. Silvery dusks;
Departing horses of December light;
White scrolling smokes of ashen emptiness,
The starlight raining down like entropy;
All the world altering till cold seemed all.

The State's greatcoats and famished dogs
Carved into us their core
Ferocities of the political.
                            Stan Laurel:

> *"Komm Ich nach Haus.*
> *Wo denn liegt Sie?"*

Sacrificium of flies.
Fleigentod of ancient witnesses.
Eyesight and cigarettes guttering.
Recalling.
Unrecalled.

Where does it begin? The gradual stoop,
Bald stasis, vertigo, the rote decline.
Percepts soften, scramble. Diapasons of ash.

Murder: this is our world. The world of flight.
In the black water, silvery human fish
Slipping away, never to return.
The cold, the wind, the evening. *Ostsektor.*

Ennui devolves to *führerprinzip:*
The rabid leap, this metamorphosis
To centipede from man, this Fall, it is
Gadarene closure to the sloth that grips
Soul in obese paralyses; that strips
Sensibility to sense, logos to hiss,
Agape to pyre.
          The gloved hand is
That from which the falcons scream and slip.

> *What comes to be decays:*
> *We render what is due.*
> *All flesh is slain, and slays;*
> *Gods have no tongue.*

Misere nobis.

Remember, Prinzessin, instead
That day free of all time?
The insect's creep along the thorn's whorled spur?
The fencing rooms, the sunlit mezzanines?
The swans outside the panes of palace glass?
Strong and cool, dear benefactor,
Dark black roses in your fingers?
I loved that look, that *hurt* look, in your eyes.

O when I knew you loved me, then I won;
I knew I was the stronger one.

      Clever memory.

The counterpoint to the moment of a death
Is white, abjuring man.
O whisper *pax*;
Bray *pax pax pax*, but everything must go:
Fissured imperium, threnodies of spines,
Dharma and blitzkrieg, baring all Sheol,
Smudging all certitude to mezzotint
Wane of totality. Grunt your crass *mot juste*,
Your tractates of phalloi: nocturne-faring theme
For unaccompanied harmonium.
Scatter of pigeons in such late quartets,
Where all the ravages of broken sunlight
Pry savage grief. Elizabethan, senex:
Be Elizabethan. Faggots' char
Finds favor with the seraphs of the left.
You wail? You wail, but take the Turing Test
Regardless, failing; light's blind signature

Re-engineering Shoah, for the world
Is all that is the case.
And the undeniable masters of the world.

Agony in the garden. He descends.
Conspiracy theorist? No, not I; not I.
Pallas; James Burnham; Gilles de Rais; not I;
The Party would be ever so displeased –
La Belle Dame Sans Maurras and Klamm and down
And down will come baby, cradle and all:

Finis.

No more peregrination, Prospero.
No sonatinas, strophe, nor Goldengrove;
The tinder sway of gristle's clock
Remitting all throes, all derelict estate,
All anomie, coherence, scattering:

Finis.

Theodicy and logorrhea wholly
Splintering as you smear to palimpsest;
The gut and cockroach spasm of mnemonic
Embracing glissandos of zero,
Slanting sans sigh into coiffures of waves
Of the charred river.

Finis.

And so the chaste skin flares into curt bark:
Earlier coltish flight slows, wanes, and grey
Flesh cranes to tendril, spurts of sprig shoot, shark
Teethbursts of branchlets, sudden leaf, swift spray
Of foliage, the heels in stiff root shod.

And I hurled your locket into the pond,
The radiant, the incorruptible water,
Under the spreading chestnut tree,
Under the aftertaste of our conspiracy,
After I betrayed you, and you me,
Along the winter rivers of the Rhine,
The pony's hoofs dotting the snow,
Heilige Nacht of epicanthic folds.

III

Marionettes

Tell me, Loki, *hammerklavier*
On the four walls of will: why are my hands cold?
Leaves clatter, warped by feeling; lynx, wasp, silk;
Inebriate postures in a dove-grey light.

Kaputt? What of it? Eras sans art are bracing.
Grünewald's iris, film of milky white,
Staring at a conception of *Das Ich*
Whose gashes issue from our smoky mouths.
Birds in the sky
Birds in the air
Tell of murders past;
But their singings cease.
Odin, let them sleep:
Prismatic night light, stage-set megaphones,
Arrange the ash reception of the bones
Of clinquant Ashkenazi.
                      Loki, Terman --
           Why are my hands cold?

Der stille Gott
Die Blauen Lider
Senkt.

Stalin
To De Gaulle: "In the end, the only victor is death."

Indifferently we drift toward jasmine shores,
Forgotten names falling over everything. Futile struggle
Of morose dolls, leather-strapped and stockinged:
Snow White. Red Riding Hood. Grin of Alice.

Epiphany: a serpent of one's own.
Chalice and debacle and asphodels.
And everything forgotten.
Tukhachevsky, Katyn,
Stauffenberg, Richtofen;
The occasional Gentile in the oven.
Gone, the calvaries, the airborne flak,
The firelit V2 attack,
Zhukov smashing pitted steel to piss,
The Son of Man, the poems of Hölderlin
In the soldier's corpse's scarlet backpack.

We dreamed of various futures. Now
We dwell in one. It is
Not what we had anticipated.
C'est la guerre.

Complete: the dotage of our nothingness:
Velocity, *c'est moi, nous sommes* – what bliss.
Atoms shattered, genomes dribbled,
Man's garbled epitaph half-scribbled
On Earth's fierce clean plutonium hull

By ants' footfalls, claw-pincers,
An insect's sibilant stroll.

Now darkness comes.
Or is it light?
The wings of understanding
Are not white.

IV

The Palace of Bells

To The One Engaged:

'Madly in love *we glittered with genitalia*.
'Kisses all Plexiglas, *acrid with ardor*,
'Liquefied, intervals *fleshed with forgetfulness*,
'Vicious and lyrical *slumbering excrescences*

'(O *apertures* optimal)
'Twist *and fly open*
'Like windows *out onto*
'The heart's *darling spirochetes*,
'Mucous all *Mayerling*,
'*Gasping* and moonlit

'To wince *as your fingertips*
'Hiss *ill arachnids*
'(*Mien* unimaginable)
'*Valiant* and pubic';

And then, ascending
Without a word,
My *princely girl*
Takes out her sword

Striking each suitor
Down in their pride.
Open your heart,
Rose bride, my bride.

V

The Tungsten Egrets

In time we tore down the last blood-encrusted cities.
The ornate tors, the mental villages. The nests
Of metal squealed and fell with biological intricacy.
Of course there was resistance. But
If mercenaries paused, we blinded them quickly,
And fretting martyrs' tongues
                              were turned to clockwork.

The camps soon choked with them, like stacked sardines;
And when the time came and the snowflakes settled,
Each prisoner was slowly turned to toys
And thrown aside, onto the rusted sidewalks.

I thought of these discordant artisans
As I was passing the other day,
By the Palace of Bells, and came upon one such plaything.
It took the labor of six years to make.
You slid a penny in the chink of it
And a jade ballerina in the center
Stilted into mathematic waltzing
As an ephemeral toccata jingled.
About its sides, twin hosts–clown cavalry–
Maneuvered in a pincer, and bell-ringers
Pulled no string at the bottom of no steeple
Which held no bell, as doll personae, royal,
A King and Queen in Fabergé carriage grandly
Waving mechanically gestured.

The Age of Steel   99

                              Wherefore I ground
Their heads in my metal teeth;

As overhead the tungsten egrets cawed,
Their tungsten talons honed
Well in eternal Rome.

And Sakura's kind father, waving
Challenged me to a later game of Go
                    (He is *quite* kind, you know)
          At his home in Hokkaido
Where Sakura lay on her belly
Licking American jelly
Watching the DVD player
(An episode of 'Buffy The Vampire Slayer')
Murmuring Catholic prayer.
Exquisite, unaware,
Till I whispered in her ear:

"You swoon amid your dreaming hair,
Grave girl, with your unnerving blackthorn eyes.
What is it that pursues you there?
                              A verdigris
Presentiment of laminate pinfolds?
Tossed veined shawls with stipplings of spun gold?
Remember, beyond the nodding paths, worm cairns;
The stroke of rowers,
                    easy in the swell,
Freshening the shallows, shoals asplash
          With herons
                    and larksong

The light-fringed reaches ebbing away, away:
Your breast a maenad's trace;
Eyes fathomless, adrowse like rondelays;
The exquisite darknesses gathering
Asseverations of the coming dusk."

Fins fled into the cradling flickering hollows
    And silently we knew
        Behind a span of bullet-proof windows, men
            Were placing the barrels of their rifles
              To rows of bowed foreheads.

    Heimdall's horn:
  In the forest hear it blow.
It pleases us to drive in sleighs
    Across deep snow.

    Baldur, the air
Is once more bright and clear,
Now Midgard is no more
    And Thule nears.

VI

Annunciations

The ailanthus world. Dream arms by right.
The slats ascending, scratching slants of gold.
The brave, resplendent, preying queues of light;
The yet to be incarnate days of old.

Prey was the dirk, the *twist*. We would indulge
Ridiculous augurs in such mortal dreams—
Prince Hamlet gurglings, abreactive sludge;
Discourse to blind the unacknowledged screams

Where Heaven breaks all the jewel of the world.
We could not turn away. To dream was quarter
To enter, eyes sun-burst with scrolls of gold,
Though the foundation stone and towers tottered.

Blood-eddies intermingled in collage
With steel: this is the title of our age.
World of the Fauves, wherein all planes collapse
Upon the disjunct features' profanation.

Engineering the final strontium
                       erasure of being
     where the howl of sun wakes forever.

O bodies, turn to air—

Annunciations, ogres, icon, time –
I want to go, to fall, to thrust them from me,
The negative peripatetic traces stirring
Each long-ceased possibility, like an eye
That seeks to seal, and judge; to gut, to sever.
Decomposition in these things lives;
And I, *essentia* of nothing. I,
Who know only unknowing.

Die laughing. This is the way it has to happen.
The time the night absorbs the day is near,
Unraveling, spattering you with ghosts of stars.

Crying child I cry
To the less devoured:
With, without,
Within, without,
Proceed.
Forward, upwards, sideways, circling,
Circling backwards, onwards, back:
Proceed.
This good lie guided me.
Remember it in tranquility. Remember
With horror. Judging historicity
All smudge and canker.
Es ist genug, genug.
Remember.
Forget.

No more of that, no more of now and then.
Of when and as, of if, seizures of if;

For the rain is beating on the windows
And I have let myself cry openly,
Stations that cry openly;
Saying to all that there is no defense,
That there is no forgiveness, saying
Thank you. Thank you dear friends kind sir
Dear mademoiselle. Thank you.
The interstellar reaches are so long –
Surely angels weary, stagger, fall.
Eye that seeks to seal, to judge, to sever.
Adders and serpents.
Thank you so much.

Proceed.

VII

Versailles

> *Spires askew*
> *Voices charring*
> *Gardens of fire*
> *Flickering swarming*

Dead selves. My own, dead years ago:
Ephemeral constructions like the others;
Cast to the sparkling, never-melting, snow.

> *Light darkens what we see.*
> *As bright as the mask on*
> *The essence seems to be,*
> *That exoskeleton*
> *Lacks all conformity*
> *To that below.*

Yet such *soirées*! Do you remember how
That motley of shadows slipped from room to room,
Whispering in claques? Or the star-gazing
Chairman's processionals of nebulae?
The duelist, aloof blade in her hand?
Sibylline youths and Nibelungen hoisting
Obese machine-pistols to scour the Lamb?
The dim forms scuttling
Coffins of marionettes beneath the rose-
seal to basement crematoria?

As voyeur X-rays bare
The armatures of grin,
Lobe, cartilage, and structure
Apparent under skin,
Flesh falls away to glare
Of goblin bone.

One evening you were assigned to me.
One night at your home you made me tea
And you and I spoke of Eternity,
As sand in the hourglass ran.

"Love is God-like," you confessed,
A cruciform design upon your left breast,
"But it is weak. And so we dream of steel."

> *what dwellingplaces? only*
> *tatters of historicity,*
> *a cry that is almost*
>
> *human*

Under Godzilla and the squids
Where the crabs have ate the lids
See the limbs unfold unfold
Is that lace that was his nose? And if
It rains, the ivory men impress
A knock upon the door

> *rags of torn light,*
> *a sheen of cranes*
> *velocity, dreamwreckage–*
> *a fistful of microseconds:*

Which passed.

We stood outside rococo gates
Watching the marble buildings burn
We heard the princes and princesses, screaming,
                    Grimaces through the smoke;
Ripe torches streaming sulfur plumes, unfleshed
Fire-tattered leaf-like pirouettes a-spin,
Opening the door, to the arena, to the Gate,
Breaking through the doors of Eternity.

And through those veils of flame you looked at me,
You looked at me, exquisite creature,
Inexplicable beauty in your every feature,
Versailles around us, burning. Versailles, burning.

Spires askew
Voices charring
Gardens of fire
Flickers swarming
Writhing
Twisting
Falling
Falling
Falling

VIII

On the Way to Utopia

Game Over.
Reboot.
Initialize.
Begin.

There: the departing ships. After the crash
Somehow we escaped detection. I don't know
How. Expression unnecessary. We must go;
Though in a sense we always have been here—
Survivors of the one enormous eye,
Whose memories of the future still betray us.
We walk out now upon the only shore.
On the way to Utopia, things happen.

Seagull parabolae, fresh sands and days:
The body grudges, gnarled by curvature
Of space, of thought, the iron cold of time,
New dissonance of sinew. So it proves
For whom it was a weariness to dare,
Leaving on time no vivid signature.
Who understands such times?
They spurn interpretation.
Memory, if all moments
Are now, what changes?

Arjuna, draw your sword, and bleed:

The bombers climb the throbbing air,
Slavering cartwheel petrol.
Children cringe in cracks and stare,
Insectoid, mewling, mortal,
And on and on they come, they come,
In agonal regalia
Unholstering metal dissonances,
And Death's genitalia. Thin gasps
And whispers, lies, proceed,
Clop-clop, down endless Escher stairs;
These desert realms, these foreign sands --
The powers, terrors, abattoirs,
And furtive plans;
All the world a screen and all the screen,
A vertigo of pixels,
Unsecular grafitti,
Engirding n*ihilismus:*
Coquetry of the Orwellian
Apocalyptic endgame;
Everyone someone else,
One quite unknown.
E Pluribus Unum.
The sea will come, will go. I carry on.

Sometimes I think on how
The girls carrying the roses looked away.
From the sense of a precipice even they knew.
For were they not as ourselves,
Paralyzed as the great doors shut behind us?
Saccharine plagency. We should have gone
To Koba's funeral in our outsized greatcoats

The Age of Steel

And leaned against the skulking portal, laughing,
Sleeves running with gore and tears.

                                  It was not so;
The paroxysm lasts no more than moments;
But brute unravelling silence like the voices
Of crows, blue-black, rubied with drying blood,
Endures. The hangsman's last
Phantasmagoria.

If we dared go beyond, where would we go?
Shrug, child. You could not have done it either.

I hate the sound of rain.
Such an empty sound,
Shrouding my ghost.
Trailing its lace across my prostheses
As I thought nonetheless
Of the torment we had penetrated,
The emblems desecrated.

> *The end of days shall hone*
> *To crystal clarity*
> *That serpentscape of sins*
> *God must forever see.*

The brutish architectures we endeavored
To sanctify with our complicity
Were the deforming mechanisms;
Squalid chalices of lugubrious wine
Staining their golem lesions on the tongue,
Spilling a new and artificial blood

Neither logic nor calculation
But a mirage that vanished as one neared.
Outside those scalene scalpels one could scry
The discord of a momentary grace;
An animated place.

But that was in another country.
And besides the wench is dead.

O shards of light that dance upon a jewel,
Is not the light upon the jewel whole?
Galaxies in a falling leaf
Beyond the shores of here.
Perhaps.
For others.

But until then
The knock
Upon the door.

Do not talk to me of restoration.
The ends the sun and sea and noon have wrought
(No remnants can be gathered)
I can no longer suffer
Nor the blackened garden
Desiring at this last
Only descriptions of the time destroyed,
Serpentine or crystalline marbles
Of that which is gone.

Shadows decomposing
All degrees of nobility and degradation.
Desolate Ninevah.

Bind it where it loosens,
Stay it where it inclines,
Fatality comes at last.

Ignorant ravage? It is vain to speak.
It is no more, and that which eagles father,
Evening shall pull down, in prolonged travail—
The morning, the starlit sky, the ceaseless
Fever.

IX

Time, Forward

Galactic coldness. Then red heat collects
In the cerebral cortex. Genesis:
Primal intoxicants stoke remonstrance,
Cracks in the structure of the bone. Influx
Agonal. Final Stage: Golem thresholds,
Cruciform loci of new integrations,
Assault of impressions. *O currite noctis equi!*
Atoms divesting all their metal birds;
Pallas in her Gorgon-headed breastplate.
Retournons a là Grand' Mère. And in the distance,
Ships from the Scythian, the Europan seas.
Greet you, Alcestis neither pale nor faint.
Awake. *Time forward*, little pioneer.

TIMELIKE CURVES

Vast the suns, the seas, the canonical sky;
Imperious as the grave, the cross, the dead,
As querulous nothingness baring its abyss:
This finitude. Take heart: such termini,
Like fog, will lift; our days, our Auschwitz, verge;
Gulls spiral soft away in timelike curves
Through all of space, unveiling a parable.
Come disembark into the end of words.

ABOUT THE AUTHOR

Correspondence directed to the author of *The Age Of Steel* should be sent via:

www.pascaleditions.com/rudimatic

NOW AVAILABLE OR COMING SOON
FROM PASCAL EDITIONS

REAP

FINAL MERCY

HARD BOP

A RENAISSANCE PATRICIAN

TERRIBLE SWIFT SWORD

THE PROBLEM WITH ZERO

CRITICAL NLP

www.pascaleditions.com
AVAILABLE ON AMAZON.COM

www.ingramcontent.com/pod-product-compliance
Lightning Source LLC
Chambersburg PA
CBHW031449040426
42444CB00007B/1030